T0148711

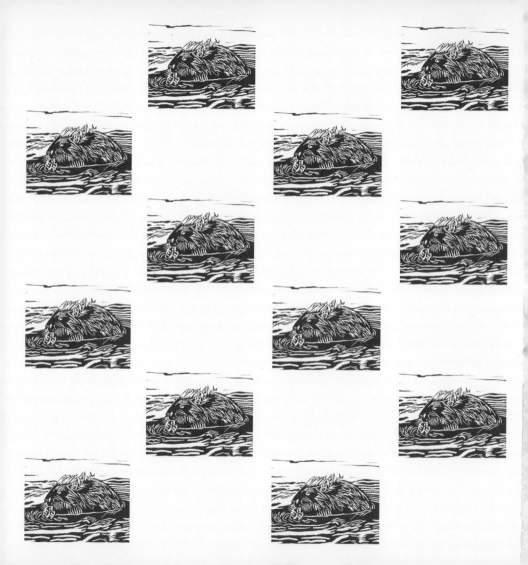

The Beaver Book

by Hugh Warwick

Series editor Jane Russ

GRAFFEG

Dedication

To Zoe and the kits – Mati and Pip.

Contents

What is a Beaver?

What is a Beaver?

There are two species of beaver still alive today: the Eurasian and the North American.

This book is going to focus mainly on the Eurasian animal (*Castor fiber*), though there will be some crossover, especially when it comes to folklore and mythology concerning the North American beaver, (*Castor canadensis*). The two species look very alike, so much so that they are almost impossible to tell apart in the wild. North American beavers were released into a number of Eurasian locations to restart the fur trade approximately a century ago, so while there are no Eurasian beavers in North America, *canadensis* is alive and still doing well in some parts of Europe. Genetically they are very different. It is believed that the species diverged around 7.5 million years ago.

An aside on the naming of things – the Latin names associated with species spring from the eighteenth-century scientist Carl Linnaeus. His choice for the European beaver is interesting in that the Latin for beaver is *fiber* and the Greek is *castor* – so essentially, this is a 'beaver beaver'!

A simple description of the beaver can be found in the writings of Pliny the Elder, from the first century AD, where he says, "The tail is like that of a fish; in the other parts of the body they resemble the otter; they are both of them aquatic animals, and both have hair softer than down."

COMMON BEAVER.

Heath sculp

Eurasian beaver

The two species look very alike, so much so that they are almost impossible to tell apart in the wild.

North American beaver

Beavers are large rodents – in the same taxonomic order as mice, rats and squirrels. In fact there is only one rodent bigger, and that is the capybara from South America. Beavers generally weigh in at around 20kg although some individuals can become considerably heavier. Their body is around 80cm long and their very distinctive tail, an additional 30cm.

Rodents get their name from the Latin *rodere*, which means 'to gnaw'. Their incisor teeth grow throughout their life and are ground into sharp chisel-like shapes due to the softer inner layer of dentine being worn away faster than the tough outer enamel.

The teeth of the beaver have enabled them to become amazingly well adapted for life as one of nature's most formidable engineers. The combination of four large, orange, incisor teeth with a powerhouse of muscles in the face means that they can fell trees over a metre in diameter. The orange colour comes from the enamel being rich in iron.

Again Pliny paints a dramatic picture of the potential in those teeth. "The bite of this animal is terrible; with its teeth if can cut down trees on the banks of rivers, just as though with a knife. If they seize a man by any part of his body, they will never loose their hold until his bones are broken and crackle under their teeth."

Large as beavers are, they are dwarfed by their relative from the Pleistocene, *Castoroides leiseyorum* which measured 2.5m long, weighing up to 200kg. This is around the size of a grizzly bear and was probably

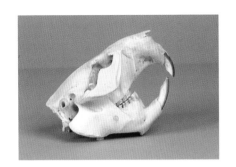

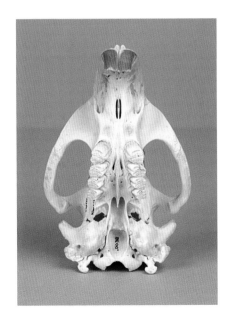

still living until around 10,000 years ago when it was swept away in an invasion by another landscape engineering species – humans.

Beavers are most at home in the water and as such are magnificently well adapted to an aquatic life. Their eyes, ears and nose are aligned so that when they swim, they can keep all their senses functioning – just above the surface of the water. They can shut their nostrils to keep water out when swimming, and have flaps of skin that help keep water out of their ears. To allow them to use their teeth underwater, for foraging and cutting wood, they can not only close their lips behind their incisors, but also shut their throat by raising the back of their tongue.

Adaptations are not restricted to the head. Large webbed feet and strong rear legs propel beavers through the water, while their forefeet are tucked up to their chest. Though juvenile beavers also use their forelegs to help in swimming.

While their tail is usually used to steer, it can also assist them when speed is needed. The beaver's tail is one of the most unusual among rodents, and mammals in general. It is paddle-shaped, covered in scales, and very functional, being used for more than just propulsion. The tail is an energy store, containing fat reserves. It helps the beaver's balance when they reach up on their hind legs to gnaw trunks. The tail is also used to help warn other beavers of potential threat – the tail-slap is a very distinctive alarm and is usually followed by a dive. For humans studying beavers, the tail has uses too – scars, nicks and notches picked up in fights can leave identifiable patterns that allow individuals to be recognized.

For insulation, beavers have a fur to die for; unfortunately this is a quite literal description as hunting for fur was a key reason for their extermination from these islands. Their fur is amazing, with two layers; guard hairs that are long and course protecting a soft, fine and dense under-fur. This lush layer helps keep water away from the skin while also trapping air to increase insulation. With up to 23,000 individual hairs per square centimetre, the beaver has over 120 times denser hair than the hairiest of humans (though still a long way short of the sea otter which has up to 400,000 hairs per square centimetre).

Beavers depend on their fur so are careful and dedicated groomers to the extent that they have evolved a comb! The second toes of the rear feet have two nails – the narrow

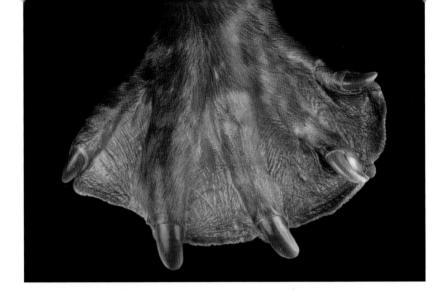

space between them allows a deep and meticulous groom.

Another aspect of beaver life that also contributed to their death is the exudate from the two castor sacs found inside their cloaca, the single sphincter-controlled opening for reproductive, urinary and digestive action. The castor sacs produce castoreum, a thick liquid that beaver use for communication, including scent marking around their territories. It was also used by people for a multitude of purposes, from medicine to food flavouring.

Beavers are herbivores, they eat vegetation; bark, shoots, and leaves. Mainly this is of deciduous trees and plants that grow in and around water. One of the great myths about beavers is that they eat fish.

This ignorance about beaver diet has serious consequences when it comes to reintroducing them into areas from which they have been eradicated. Some in the fishing community remain worried about the impact that the beaver will have on their stocks. Well, the truth is that beavers not only don't eat fish, but they also help create habitat that allows fish to flourish. Concerns tend to drift away when the fisherfolk listen to the ecologists.

What beavers eat is very tied into their role as ecosystem engineers. The beaver does not hibernate so needs to keep eating throughout the year, even when the plants it depends upon stop growing. To allow this to happen beavers need to create a reserve, and this is one of the key roles played by the lakes that form behind their famous dams.

Vegetation is harvested and stored underwater keeping it cold; so in other words beavers invented the refrigerator long before we did.

Observation of free-living beavers in Scotland shows them consuming over 70 different plant species. These range from trees such as alder, lime and oak, to herbaceous and aquatic vegetation, such as bedstraw, blackberry, knotweed, nettles and lilies. Poplars are a favourite, and species such as willow, hazel, ash and dogwood are harvested in such a way that new shoots emerge from their stumps, creating a natural coppice.

The management of the land by the beaver also encourages the species it likes to eat. While they are quite capable of felling a tree over a metre in diameter, they tend to prefer

saplings with a girth of around 5cm. This material is gathered and woven into the area surrounding the lodge or burrow which means that, even if the water freezes, they can easily access their larder of leaves and bark.

When beavers eat, they can leave very characteristic remains that serve as a useful clue when out looking for field signs of their presence. Obviously there are the distinctive chippings around the base of felled or partially felled trees. But it is the creation of lawns that is perhaps a more unexpected function of beaver feeding. These appear close to water over a period of time as the beavers emerge at night and graze. It is possible to confuse them with the sort of cropping produced by ducks and geese but those lawns will be littered with droppings and feathers.

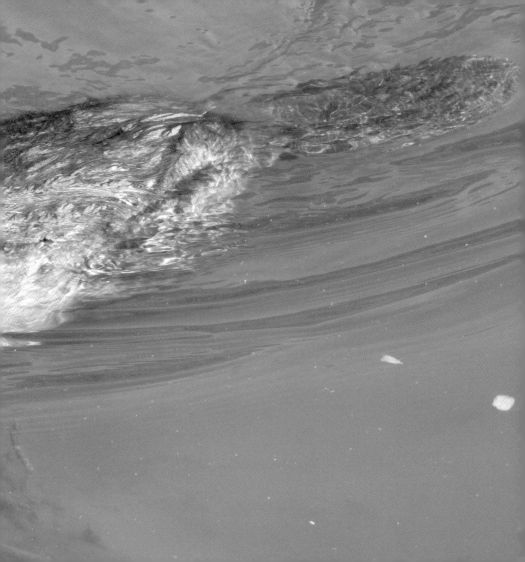

It is possible to get a clear image by looking closely at the remains of the slightly sturdier plant species, such as rushes. Here there is a fascinating similarity to the feeding remains of the much smaller rodent, the water vole, where a distinctive 45 degree cut in the stem is characteristic. Another giveaway is a beaver feeding station, again similar to that of a water vole but on a much larger scale. Rather than the 8-10cm lengths of vegetation of their smaller cousins, beavers will leave piles of debris, often de-barked and discarded sticks.

Beaver Life

Life begins with mating, of course, and for the beaver this takes place in the water. The female floats, the male clings as they mate and then, in around three months, beaver babies are born. Known as kits, there will usually be between two and four furry young. Milk is on hand for up to three months, but they are precocious eaters, consuming vegetation as well within a few days of birth.

Lodge life consists of more than just parents and newborn; older siblings will help in the rearing, joining the effort of collecting food. After a couple of months, the youngsters will start to explore, learning the rudiments of beaver life, swimming and diving around the lodge. Sometimes they will 'caravan' with one of the older relatives, swimming in their wake or clinging to their back.

Beavers build and reinforce family bonds through grooming, especially between adults and young. The young spend time in play, wrestling and establishing an understanding of hierarchy. If they become distressed or lost the young make noises – gentle squeaking, crying or mewing. Adults can and do vocalise, but less often and normally only on meeting.

This all gives the impression of a rather cosy family life; the lodge, a safe retreat, and older siblings on hand, or paw, to assist. Couple this with the fact that beaver pairs tend to remain together and it's a surprise that the animal has not become a staple of Valentine's Day greetings cards. Perhaps it is the orange teeth that have put a stop to that market. It is, of course, not as 'perfect' as it might seem.

There can be a displacement of either adult should another come along with a fancy for the location and the mate.

After two years of learning and then teaching, the young disperse to find their own space. Beavers are territorial and will actively defend a territory. Fights are common with individuals from other family groups; these can result in serious injuries from bites to the body and tail, and can result in death. Sometimes the adolescent beavers need a bit of encouragement to move on from their natal territory when they have reached the age to find their own patch.

Dispersal distances from the birth lodge can vary, dependent on conditions and the density of beavers in the area. The juvenile beaver may take up residence just down river or might have to go as far as 50km to find the perfect new home.

Beaver Engineering

A dam may well be considered a defining creation of the beaver, but they are not always required. The purpose of the dam is to create a pond for food storage and security. Beavers need water at least a metre deep. They much prefer slow-moving water with a gentle gradient. If a beaver is living somewhere that already has a lake or pond, or the river is large and the banks are friable, then the dam may be unnecessary.

When a dam is required, beavers are adept at using what they find. Logs, either felled for the purpose or found elsewhere, are woven into a structure with mud and stone, twigs and other vegetation. The upstream side of the dam usually has a layer of silt and soil compacted into it, ensuring the structure remains robust and extremely hard-wearing.

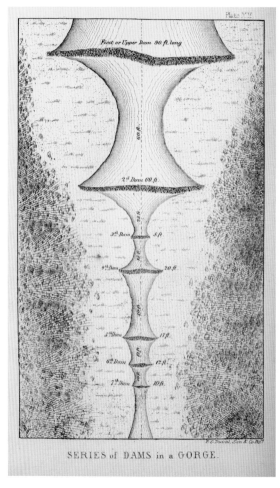

Plate VII

First or Upper Dam 90 ft. long

60 ft.

2ᵈ Dam 60 ft.

5ᵗʰ Dam   8 ft.

4ᵗʰ Dam   20 ft.

5ᵗʰ Dam   17 ft.

6ᵗʰ Dam   12 ft.

7ᵗʰ Dam   10 ft.

SERIES of DAMS in a GORGE.

Series of Dams in a Gorge, *The American Beaver and His Works* by Lewis H. Morgan, 1868.

Right: Photos of Beaver Dams from *Annual report 10th;11th;12th* (New York State Forest, Fish and Game Commission) (1904-1906).

PART OF A BEAVER DAM 250 FEET IN LENGTH.

DAM CONSTRUCTED OF LARGER STICKS. Photos by W. H. De Graff.

With the risk of drifting into myth, the description given by Gerald of Wales, writing at the end of the twelfth century AD, gives a fascinating, if erroneous insight into the engineering abilities of the beaver. "The beavers, in order to construct their castles in the middle of rivers, make use of the animals of their own species instead of carts, who, by a wonderful mode of carriage, convey the timber from the woods to the rivers. Some of them, obeying the dictates of nature, receive on their bellies the logs of wood cut off by their associates, which they hold tight with their feet, and thus with transverse pieces placed in their mouths, are drawn along backwards, with their cargo, by other beavers, who fasten themselves with their teeth to the raft."

Beaver Lodge, Grass Lake from *The American beaver and his works* by Morgan, Lewis Henry, 1868.

Section of Great Beaver Dam, Grass Lake from from *The American beaver and his works* by Morgan, Lewis Henry, 1868.

Gerald of Wales continues with a rather eloquent description of the results of this labour. "In some deep and still corner of the river, the beavers use such skill in the construction of their habitations, that not a drop of water can penetrate, or the force of storms shake them; nor do they fear any violence but that of mankind, nor even that, unless well armed. They entwine the branches of willows with other wood, and different kinds of leaves, to the usual height of the water, and having made within-side a communication from floor to floor, they elevate a kind of stage, or scaffold, from which they may observe and watch the rising of the waters. In the course of time, their habitations bear the appearance of a grove of willow trees, rude and natural without, but artfully constructed within."

Streams can also become blocked through the natural accumulation of debris, and these 'dams' could at first glance be confused for beaver constructions. However, a brief

examination will show an absence of distinctly beaver-cut stems and a lack of upstream smoothing.

Where the land is fairly flat, the building of a dam can just move the flow of water rather than stop it. The beaver will continue to pursue construction until there is enough of a change in the gradient to provide a boundary for a pond. This can result in dams extending hundreds of metres through boggy terrain. These constructions are easily robust enough to tolerate use as a path for people. Archeological evidence in parts of the Somerset levels suggests that beaver dams once formed wetland trackways which linked early communities.

The lodges, so delightfully described by Gerald of Wales, are not the only lodgings beaver make. They are excellent burrowers and will make homes underground should the gradients of the surrounding banks ensure they can dig up and away from the water, to keep living space dry when water levels rise.

While it is the lodges, dams and their corresponding ponds and wetlands for which the beaver is most celebrated, they do engineer another, often dramatic, change to the landscape. Access to water is important to a beaver, it is part of their survival strategy. When threatened they dive and swim. However, not all their food is found conveniently beside the water, so they have developed a cunning strategy to cope with the need to forage further. They take the water to the food.

Digging canals into the landscape, often radiating from the main pond, allows the beavers both to travel safely to forage, and also to transport wood more easily (though not by using their compatriots as carriages!) Sometimes these might be the result of regular journeys wearing a path which then fills with water. But they also excavate and then manage specific canals, ensuring that vegetation and sediment do not clog their artery. Most are quite short, just a few metres – but some reach over 150 metres into the surrounding landscape. The management of these canals extends to ensuring, in dry spells, that water is retained, so they build small dams to the 40-50cm wide channels, adding to the great ecological impacts these engineers have when they take up residence.

The dams, ponds and canals, coupled with the continual disturbance through harvesting vegetation and moving branches to the water, means that the beaver creates an 'untidy' landscape. If beavers built a dam, creating a pond, and then just left, the ecological returns would not be as valuable.

Instead, what the beaver does is generate one of the most sought-after landscapes. They promote heterogeneity, the mishmash of habitats that result from their hard work. This patchiness and complexity really is ecological gold. One of the greatest threats wildlife faces throughout the country, and indeed, around the world, is homogeneity – the monocultures of single species plantations and fields, and the overarching desire for complete control. Ecological restoration relies on breaking through the monotony and giving diversity the chance to flourish. Diversity also brings resilience.

Research from the University of Stirling found that when beavers were present there were 33% more species of plant and 26% more invertebrates in the affected landscape. These changes then created increased populations of fish and waterfowl.

Yet beavers do more than create ecological diversity, they also help to undo some of the other detrimental effects of human activity. Eutrophication, the increase in nutrients in the waterways of the country, may superficially sound like a good thing. After all, nutrients are crucial – without them we die. Ecology is not so simple, as the

artificial rush of nutrients into our waterways is suffocating the life out of them. Certain species flourish, like algae, and these can smother the water, preventing light from reaching the plants that generate the oxygen that keeps the animals alive. Having a beaver dam helps to reduce this flood of pollutants, most of which come from agricultural run-off. Researchers have found a 50% reduction in phosphorous and 44% decline in nitrates below beaver dams. And as the water is held back by dams, allowing the pollutants to settle out, there is also a reduction in the flow of water during storm events. The Cornwall Beaver Project found that dams reduced peak discharges by nearly 50% – reducing the risk of flooding downstream.

Couple all this with the evidence that beaver wetlands act as a carbon store, thus increasing our ability to reduce the impact of a changing climate, then it is a wonder that the species is not at the forefront of environmental policy! The data are impressive, while dry grassland soils can store 40-100 tonnes of carbon per hectare, in old and abandoned beaver meadows this rises to 3-400 tonnes and in active beaver meadows it is up to a startling 1,400 tonnes.

Water storage is not all about mitigating flooding. In our increasingly erratic climate the need to store water as drought mitigation can be just as important. Beavers slow, store and spread water in the landscape – increasing reserves for times of drought.

People and Beavers

There is evidence of humans in Britain from nearly a million years ago; footprints from what is thought to be *Homo antecessor*. These early humans would have shared the land with two species of beaver, *Trogontherium* – the Giant Beaver – and 'our' European beaver. The Giant Beaver seems to have vanished around 400,000 years ago.

Other than bone, the earliest evidence of beavers in Britain comes from some wood that shows distinctive tooth marks and was found, somewhat incongruously, in Stoke Newington, north London. This was chewed in the early Pleistocene, commonly referred to as the Ice Age, over a million years ago.

The climate fluctuated dramatically over the millennia with ice sheets advancing and retreating, periodically pushing both beavers and people out of Britain. It was not until around 13,500 years ago that conditions were mild enough to allow sufficient vegetation to flourish to entice beavers back, along with people.

The relationship between beavers and people is more complex than it might at first be thought. This was not just a predator/prey situation; beavers seem to have been far more important to people. For example, an excavation of a Mesolithic site in the Vale of Pickering, north Yorkshire, has revealed a wooden platform that seems to have been built to support human activity in a marshy area. And among the wooden stems are many that are beaver-gnawed, suggesting that this was built upon a beaver lodge or dam, incorporating the materials.

Throughout the Mesolithic, beaver territories will have been sought out as they provided not just potential building materials, but also a ready source of animals to hunt – not necessarily the beavers. The ponds and the clearings with new vegetative growth will have attracted grazing and browsing species.

Along the Thames there is plenty of archaeological evidence of people settling into beaver territories from the Mesolithic onwards. Neolithic farmers seem to have concentrated their activities within 50 metres of the tributaries, the same area the beavers would use. It is likely that people were attracted to the combination of cleared space, thanks to the harvesting work of the beavers, and the fertile soils accumulated in beaver ponds. Additionally, the browsing potential of the coppiced trees would have been a draw.

It is also not unreasonable to think of beavers as teachers. It will not have escaped our ancestors' notice that here was an animal that could manage water; that was able to build structures that could act as causeways through wetlands; that engineered canals to transport logs; that introduced them, perhaps, to the idea of coppicing, and also showed how decaying plant matter could enrich the soil.

The image of the admirably busy beaver is fine, but it is very possible we are underplaying the significance of this amazing rodent.

In more mundane fashion, beavers were also a source of food. Humans have probably been the principle predator of beavers for thousands of years. There is about as much meat on a beaver as on a roe deer, so it was a valuable source of food, especially in late winter when other animals were harder to hunt. Evidence from the butchery marks on beaver bones from the Mesolithic to the Iron Age support this. Recipes from the Middle Ages show they were still being eaten, but by this stage rarely and by the very rich. In the mid-fifteenth century the *Boke of Nurture* was published, containing a recipe for beaver tail as a Lenten food – evidence again of the strange fishy reputation of this mammal. Though the 'Wild Beaver Pies' on offer at Brockleby's, Melton Mowbray, owe more to the Vale of Belvoir than to the rodent... in fact it is a steak and ale pie. Although Belvoir is pronounced 'beaver'; it is unrelated as 'Belvoir' comes from the Norman invasion and translates as 'beautiful view'.

Above: 'Wild Beaver Pies' on offer at Brockleby's, Melton Mowbray.

Above: Shigir Idol, Regional Museum of Local Lore, Yekaterinburg, Russia.

These engineers found their mortal remains being put to use as well; in particular, the lower jaw makes an effective woodworking tool. Those teeth can still function after death. The spectacular Shigir Idol, thought to be the oldest known wooden sculpture in existence, and now housed in the Sverdlovsk Regional Museum of Local Lore, Yekaterinburg, Russia, was carved using tools made from the teeth of beavers around 12,000 years ago.

Clearly their fur was also very important. Archaeological evidence comes from the characteristic skinning marks left on bones. And there was the discovery at the Sutton Hoo excavation of the seventh century AD Anglo Saxon ship burial in Suffolk, of what is interpreted as the remains of a beaverskin bag that had once held a lyre.

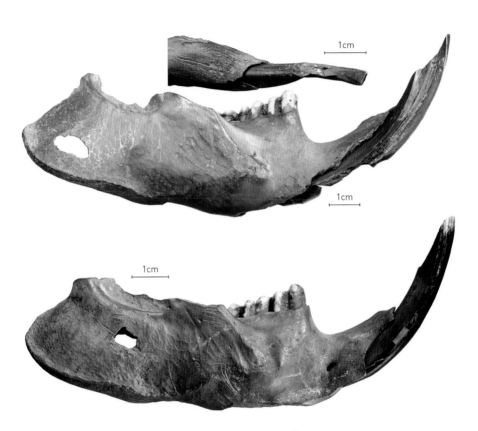

Lower jaw of a beaver, used as a woodworking tool
from mesolithic (7000 BC), wetland site Zamostje,
Upper Volga region, Russia.

The fur was so highly valued that there is legislation from the tenth century in Wales that refers to the fur being used to trim the King's clothes. And evidence of the trade can be seen in Acts of Parliament imposing tolls on the export of beaver skins in the twelfth century.

Given humanity's regular extermination of life it may be naive to think that this species, so valuable as an engineer and for fur, might have been spared that fate. Archaeologist Bryony Coles suggests that, "...as humans developed their own skills as water engineers, from the later Middle Ages onwards, they came increasingly to see beavers as a nuisance rather than as a living package of valuable commodities. The people who invested time and money in the development of water meadows or canals would not have wanted beavers to move in."

This is perhaps why the beaver was entered as vermin into the *Acts for the Preservation of Grayne* when it was passed in the mid-sixteenth century. There is a fascinating but deeply depressing book written by Roger Lovegrove called *Silent Fields* in which he charts the persecution of wildlife caught up as vermin and recorded in parish records around the country as people applied for the bounties on nature's head. From these records the last beaver killed was in 1789, on the River Wharfe between Leeds and York. Though traditionally their extermination from England and Wales has been dated in the twelfth century, and in Scotland in the sixteenth century.

If the date pulled from the parish records is to believed then it is unlikely this was the last British beaver, and there may have even been individuals that lasted into the nineteenth century. The animal that was once abundant was driven to extinction by humanity's greed – the greed for fur and castoreum, and the greed of not being able to share space.

Beavers did not vanish entirely from Britain, however. They can still be found in the names given to places that at one time would have been associated with the real thing.

The Bar Brook in Derbyshire, about ten miles south west of Sheffield, used to be dammed, by people, creating the Barbrook Reservoir. The Saxon word for beaver is 'bar' and this would be a stream that was once naturally impounded by the animal. The expert eye of beaver breeder and author Derek Gow reveals this as a once heavily beavered landscape. In his magnificent book, *Bringing Back the Beaver* he writes, "...their past existence remains etched in an intricacy of the pattern left by the water's wanderings as it slewed and shifted a millennia ago in an ineffectual effort to bypass their dams."

The Beaver Inn is upstream from Westward Ho! and has taken its title to heart, filled with iconography of its namesake. The Inn has been in Appledore for over 400 years and its name has rather disturbing origins. Apparently it was the pub in which the Press Gang would gather prior to 'volunteering' innocents into the King's service. The Press Gang were noted for their uniform of beaver felt

MONEY POUCH MADE OF TANNED KITTEN BEAVER'S TAIL.
SLIGHTLY REDUCED.

hats, and so the pub became known as the place of the beavers – and the name stuck. It is also possible that the name stemmed from Appledore and nearby Bideford being trading ports for ships coming from the New World, whose crews would bring with them beaver skins and other new and exciting goods.

The Beverley Brook runs through Richmond Park, reaching the Thames at Barn Elms. Bevercotes in Nottinghamshire had a colliery, now disbanded, which has been returned to woodland – maybe one day the beavers will return? Then there are Beverley in Yorkshire, which also has a pub called The Beaver, Beverston in Gloucestershire and Beverton on Exmoor.

Pop over the Firth of Forth and turn right towards Kirkcaldy and you will come to the Beverkae Roundabout. It is an entirely unprepossessing junction between the A909 and the B925 that is not worthy of much thought other than it being a reminder of what used to be.

There is a Beaver Pool, just down from the Beaver Bridge, near Betws y Coed in north Wales. Place names that capture the animal in Welsh, *afangc*, can also be found in the beautiful valley in Snowdonia, Nant Francon, which means Vale of the Beaver.

Some of the references may have as much to do with the products made from the beavers as the beavers themselves. The Hat and Beaver pub in Leicester, closed in 2007, will have been a reference to the millinery as much as the mammal.

reference in Chaucer's *Canterbury Tales* where he wrote of "A merchant was there with a forked beard / In motley, and high on his hose he sat, / Upon his head a Flandrish beaver hat." Motley refers to a multicoloured clothing, Flandrish being Flemish.

The felting process required the separation of the long guard hairs from the softer under-fur – which is why old beaver coats were prized as this process had already been done, so in fact the best way to get your beaver felt was through recycling. The shorter hairs were then shaved free of the skin and pummelled and boiled until they combined together into a dense felt, when they could then be placed over a 'form' and pressed into hats.

In fact hats were the closest most people got to beavers in the UK from the sixteenth to nineteenth century. Beaver hair could be felted into a soft yet resilient product that made for wonderful hats. There is an early

From Wolfgang Helmhardt von Hohberg's 'Georgica curiosa',
instructions for agriculture and housekeeping.

The remains of this industry can be seen in the coat of arms of the town of Denton, now part of Greater Manchester and once a centre of the industry.

The demand for beaver fur nearly exterminated the beavers of Europe. There is an argument that they only survived thanks to the discovery of a seemingly inexhaustible supply of beavers in the New World, so the cost of trapping the remaining few was undercut by nature's trans-Atlantic bounty.

There were active efforts to protect the dwindling European beavers. In 1845 Norway became the first country to legislate for their protection. This resulted in a pocket of Scandinavian beavers being saved. Sweden was slightly behind the curve on this, banning hunting in 1873, two years after the last Swedish beaver had been killed.

By the late nineteenth century there were relic populations totalling just 1200 individuals throughout Europe. There were estimated to be 200 on the River Elbe in Germany and around 30 on the Rhone in France. Hunting regulation brought some respite and allowed populations to grow again.

Denton Coat of Arms from *Denton The Official Handbook* at Tameside Local Studies & Archives.

Beaver Reintroductions

In continental Europe, plans to reintroduce beavers began in 1922 in Sweden. There followed other projects including Bavaria in 1966 and Romania in 1988. But the UK remained resistant.

By the 1990s there was discussion in Scotland about a formal release experiment and trial was suggested for 2000. However, the UK Government said no.

It was not until 2008 that the go ahead was given for the first official release of beavers, in Knapdale Forest, Argyll, and in 2009, 17 beavers from Telemark, Norway, were released into three lochs on the estate following a six month quarantine. Thus began the Scottish Beaver Trial.

There had, however, been other, less official experiments, reintroducing this remarkable rodent.

Paul and Louise Ramsay live in Bamff House, Alyth, in Perthshire. Paul inherited the estate with a view to continuing the tradition of managing livestock. But he was also driven by a deeper love of nature and, after attending meetings in the 1990s where the potential eco-engineering capacity of the long-extinct beaver was being discussed, he became very keen to see if they lived up to their potential.

Paul got fed up waiting for official sanction, so he decided to launch an experiment on his own land. At 1300 acres (over 500ha) the Bamff estate is substantial enough to support both the farming and an enclosure of beavers.

In 2002 Paul and Louise released two beavers into an enclosed section of the estate. Two families of beavers have now been breeding since 2005 and have made a significant impact on the Bamff landscape. Ditches have been converted into a series of ponds and swamps. The species that have been directly benefitting from the benevolent engineers include otters, water voles, herons, ducks, and a host of invertebrates and amphibians. Indirectly benefitting are the owls, hunting the increased abundance of small mammals, and woodpeckers, capitalising on the dead wood, home to insect larvae.

The changes were dramatic and fast. Trees were, obviously, felled as the beavers harvested the leaves. Streams were dammed, resulting in wet areas expanding as the water flow was reduced. The transformed landscape includes a 100m long dam. As the water rose behind the initial dam, the lie of the land caused it to spill around the northern edge. To stop the annoying trickle, and it is the noise that stimulates the behaviour, the dam was extended, creating a really biodiverse wetland where once was grazing.

The increased abundance and diversity of wildlife that has accompanied these industrious engineers is evidence of what is known as a trophic cascade. Where the reappearance of one species has a knock-on effect across the wider ecosystem.

On a slightly grander scale and with our beaver's cousin, the story of Yellowstone National Park in the USA gives a good insight into what this means. In the 1920s the wolves were exterminated by the federal government across the park. This led to a dramatic increase in the numbers of elk living there. The elk, without the population control exerted by the top predator, destroyed many species of tree, including willow and aspen, trees crucial to the beavers for food and dam building. This helped drive beavers from most of the park, resulting in the collapse of their dams and the ponds reverting to streams. Erosion increased, riparian vegetation was lost and with it the great diversity of invertebrate life.

In 1995 wolves were reintroduced. This caused elk numbers to decrease, and beaver colonies to become reestablished, bringing with them the re-wetting and disordering of the landscape – and the insects, birds, fish and amphibians returned,

returning the park to some of its former glory.

Maybe one day there will be a reintroduction of wolves to Scotland, but for now, they have beavers, and they have helped to create these great ecological cascades where their engineering allows so much more life to thrive.

Over time the beavers of Bamff extended their range across the estate. A ditch that runs along the low ground became 'naturalised' with dams, pools, and meanders. There are now around 40 dams and associated pools

Beaver young, kits, have been seen every year since 2007. Bamff has not only become a centre for tourism, with people coming to see the marvellous changes, but also of research, with ecologists coming to

study, and others, with rewilding in mind, come to learn.

The Ramsay beavers were not alone in that part of the world. In fact beavers were first seen in the River Tay estuary in 2001. These had come from either deliberate releases or accidental escapes. No one has owned up. These animals have been the cause of considerable consternation and have resulted in a long-running campaign from different sides of the fence.

Meanwhile, the Scottish Beaver Trial was considered a success. Following general public support, alongside consultation with the key stakeholders, the Scottish Government decided in 2016 that the beavers could stay and then in 2019, went further and granted them legal protection.

However, the presence of the less official beavers did cause concern. Conflict with some land-owners was caused when agricultural land became temporarily inundated following the damming of drainage ditches and the burrowing into flood banks.

There are ways to work with beavers in a farmed landscape. Beavers in the wrong place can be trapped and relocated. Trees that are precious can be ringed in wire. Dams can be removed. There are tried and trusted techniques. Yet just months after they were granted protection, Scottish Natural Heritage, now known as NatureScot, granted licenses to kill 87 beavers, amounting to around 20% of the country's total population. This resulted in considerable anger among conservationists and animal lovers. One of the reactions was unusual, in that it used art to express the true feelings of many about these returned animals. The project, '87Beavers: In Memoriam' has exhibited the work of campaigning artists all over Scotland.

By 2021 there were known to be more than ten beaver populations living in enclosures in the UK, and 13 projects in development, both fenced and free-living. There are populations on the Tamar River, the Stour in Kent, the Wye on the Welsh borders. The National Trust released beavers into a sheltered valley on the edge of the South Downs in 2021. There have been beavers living on the River Otter in Devon since 2008, with confirmed breeding since 2014. The initial reaction of the authorities was to remove the beavers – possibly by killing them. This was greeting with an outcry and after the beavers were trapped and given a health check, they were released back into

the wild and became the start of an important piece of research.

What followed was the River Otter Beaver Trial, the results of which, when published in 2020, concluded

that there are now at least 13 family groups living in this area. They are dispersing along the River Otter, as well as surrounding tributaries.

As would be expected, the main river has remained un-dammed. It is the smaller streams that have been impounded and even then, the overall impact is relatively small with just 1.9km of the 594km of waterways

in the River Otter catchment having dams. One sequence of dams has been recorded as generating an important reduction in peak flows of water in a downstream village. These are the sorts of flood-mitigating benefits that can occur when these natural engineers get to work.

In Bavaria, where beavers have been back for over 50 years, people understand that to prevent undesirable tree felling, using sandpaint or wire mesh can deter beavers. If flood waters rise in places where it is not appreciated, water levels can be moderated using pipes to divert water from the pond, dams can be notched down a bit, or even removed. Similar work is done in North America – given a little time the relationships between humans and beavers can change as the benefits they bring are appreciated.

Interestingly as beaver numbers have increased, so has public support. Research carried out by the University of Exeter concluded that while the return of beavers did generate some 'costs' in the form of some flooded farmland, these costs were far outweighed by the value added by ecotourism and flood alleviation. The beavers also filtered out pollutants from the river, including manure, slurry and fertilisers – all of which cause eutrophication, resulting in lower oxygen levels in the water. The beaver ponds were also found to have 37% more fish compared to other parts of the river.

Despite the clear evidence of beavers helping nature return, and of their services in pollution and flood reduction, the return of the beaver to the waterways of Britain is not without conflict. Most of this is due to ignorance or a very reasonable fear of change. The paperwork needed to claim the benefits that would come with the environmental improvements that the beavers bring is enough to put off many.

Sometimes the concerns are rather wild. For example the Game and Wildlife Conservation Trust (GWCT) published a report titled, *'Environmental engineer or waterway menace?'* They raise the concern about "attacks on dogs and even people" from the increasing numbers of these animals. A little digging can go a long way and it seems that the attack on 'people' was a reference to an incident in Belarus in 2013 where a man died of the injuries sustained from being bitten by a beaver after he tried to restrain it in order to get a photograph taken with the large rodent. In much the same way that it is important to treat all animals with respect, the return of the beaver should coincide with education. Walkers in the countryside have far more to fear from cattle than beavers.

The GWCT report also claimed that beavers could present a problem for spawning fish, that salmon and trout would find access to breeding grounds blocked by dams. This raises an interesting question as to how the species managed to coexist for so many years before the eradication of the beaver.

However a systematic meta-analysis of the scientific literature published in the journal Fish and Fisheries in 2012 should give those who wish to be guided by the science enough evidence to make up their

minds. The review showed that, "On mainstream rivers, beaver dams are rarely constructed and hence do not pose significant impediments to fish passage, a suggestion supported by the response of a large majority of the experts. Where dams do exist they are considered to be semi-permeable structures that allow a proportion of fish to pass both in the upstream and downstream direction."

It goes on to point out that while on narrow, tributary streams, dams can have an impact on fish movements when water levels are low, the impact is "short-lived and localised." Though, of course, the presence of beavers does counteract low water levels by providing pools.

The majority of the literature reviewed showed that the presence of beavers had a net positive effect. The Beaver Trust concluded: "There are numerous articles that demonstrate the benefits beavers can provide for fish. These can include increased abundance, juvenile-rearing habitat, refuge from predators, improved condition, increased growth, increased habitat diversity thus supporting a greater variety of fish species and by proxy life stages to name a few. The two main concerns that fisheries owners have are the potential for dams to block salmonid migration and the loss of spawning reeds due to damming activity. The research is divided and sometimes speculative on the extent to which dams block fish passage and this is an ongoing debate."

When it comes to managing the relationship between beavers and

people, it is important to realise this is probably more about managing people than beavers! It has been shown that around 98% of all the conflicts occur within 20m of water. If people begin to retreat from the water, if they do not take development and farming right into the riparian zone, the trouble vanishes. Furthermore, this richly biodiverse feature, the borders of waterways, gets a chance to recover from generations of human activity.

While the return of beavers to the UK has certainly attracted attention, this is a remarkably tame and gentle operation in comparison to the drama of what happened in north America. It started with the live-trapping of beavers and translocating them to where they had been wiped out. In Pennsylvania, for example, 47 pairs were released between 1915 and 1924. These settled in with vigour and by 1934 these 94 were estimated to be 15,000.

However, it was the 1948 adventure that really captured attention. First, there was a problem. After World War Two there was a need to provide housing and expansion in the Payette Lake region of Idaho set up a conflict between the incoming humans and the resident beavers. Capturing these animals and translocating them into the forested and mountainous land was hard, expensive and damaging to beavers who did not weather the long journey with any ease.

Subsequently, a quite brilliantly eccentric scheme was prepared, initially using a stunt beaver called Geronimo who was repeatedly placed in a box, put aboard a plane, and

then at around 200m above ground was thrown out – assisted, it should be added, by a surplus post-war parachute. After Geronimo had proved this could work without ill effect, the plan was put into action and 76 beavers were successfully translocated into the remoter regions of Idaho. Well, 75 – one of the beavers took a tumble when the box opened before reaching the ground.

Amazingly the beavers of north America have now re-occupied most of their former range with a nationwide population of up to 25,000,000.

Beaver Trust

Time is running out and neither political nor commercial action appears to be having any bearing on the desperate demise of wildlife and rivers across Britain. What is more, the context for recovery is about to get more challenging every year with increasing drought, rain storms, wildfire risk and temperature change, all of which put pressures on our fragile freshwater ecosystems, soils and wildlife. It is imperative we find ways to support recovery, and deploy them with serious urgency and intent; like our lives depend on it.

Astonishingly for us there is a creature slowly spreading within our rivers and streams that is nothing short of a gift in the struggle for resilience building, if we just give it space to operate. Beavers have been beautifully termed a 'hydrological and ecological Swiss army knife'

by world-leading beaver ecologist Ben Goldfarb. What is more they are formerly native to Britain until human hunting exterminated the island's population, so they absolutely belong here in our landscape. Beavers could help change the fate of our rivers, and all that depends upon them above and beneath the surface.

Keystone effects

The stealthy operating beaver's primary tool for climate action is its dam. Wherever they need to increase water depth, a strategy to improve their own ease of movement and safety, they will build impressively robust structures out of mud, stone, sticks and other foraged materials. Most often this will happen in headwaters, since downstream rivers are deeper. In doing so they slow the flow of water through the

landscape, storing and spreading it into the land beside waterways and transforming rivers back into the spongy chains of wetland habitat they used to be before humans drained and straightened them.

What happens next is the incredible part. Life returns. Beaver wetlands are a mosaic of diverse and changing habitats. Science has proven beaver ponds result in a boom in plantlife, bats, birds, insects, fish biomass

Science has proven beaver ponds result in a boom in plantlife, bats, birds, insects, fish biomass and aquatic life generally.

and aquatic life generally. The critical thing here is they support biodiversity and abundance, the latter being something we no longer look for following a generational downgrade of expectation from being 'in nature'.

But even if you aren't into wildlife, the water cycle is something everyone depends upon and again beavers are our ally here. In slowing the flow of water downstream, peak rainfall flows can be halved during storms, with water leaving beaver wetlands at a slower rate over a longer period of time, the downstream risk of flooding is significantly lowered. Something that the Environment Agency is paying hundreds of millions of pounds to try and achieve every year. Beavers not only do it for free but they'll manage

the maintenance of these flood defences as long as they are present.

Drought hasn't been at the forefront of Britain's collective minds historically, but we're facing real water shortages from here on. In the spring drought of 2020 at the Cornwall Beaver Project, situated on an organic farm, irrigation was necessary and possible from the beaver ponds onto surrounding farmland. Neighbouring farmers had no such option and suffered the drought. Once again it's beavers that offer an effective water battery, storing our life blood, water, to increase resilience.

Nor do their keystone impacts end there. Beaver dams filter pollutants and silt from the water course and the wetlands even sequester carbon when actively managed by beavers. Best of all, they create the most stunningly wild, captivating wetland spaces for us to enjoy and encounter what a thriving landscape should feel like.

Beaver Trust

With such a profoundly impactful creature comes a fear of change and loss of control. The return of beavers is necessitating science-lead discussion, policy consideration and re-education of how we can learn to live alongside them again. Beaver Trust was founded in 2019 to help support beavers' re-establishment across the country. It began as and remains a small, agile organization built on friendship and a shared urgency to restore natural landscapes.

The charity's mission is to restore Britain's rivers and wildlife with beavers, but it is not just about a single species. This systemic problem demands a systemic solution. Beaver Trust works through collaborative partnerships and aims to bring people and organizations together to help tackle the climate and ecological crises. For example, there is little point returning beavers to a river catchment where intensive farming right to the edge would mean instant conflict with dam-building, burrowing or beaver foraging. So our work extends to making rivers fit for beavers and other beneficiaries, looking at buffer zones and other measures to re-naturalize whole catchments.

We, the nature sector generally, must work proactively *with* agriculture, water companies and commercial interests, sport and game interests, the general public

and the Government to create and enact a positive vision for the future of Britain's rivers. Without a shared vision and aligned action we cannot expect improvement in the status quo.

Policy change

Beaver Trust identified the need for an English national beaver strategy to support the return of beavers to the wild and to provide a legislative framework for their management. As a core strand of work, the charity convenes collaborative discussion with a broad stakeholder base to achieve good decisions on beaver policy, management and funding. Through this work we aim to agree common principles across decisions like beaver status, licensing, sourcing, disease risk, management and animal welfare.

Beaver management

Central to any framework for beavers' return is the need for a robust management framework; a consistently applied set of guidelines by which beavers and their impacts can be managed; for example where they are not desirable. Management techniques are well established and proven to be effective, ranging from painting a sand-glue mixture as individual tree protection, or more targeted dam removal, through to removal of the animal itself and relocation to a new site.

One of the most effective methods of beaver management when issues arise, is having a rapid response. In order to do this we need to scale training and resources with the ability to manage beavers. Beaver Trust has started a network of catchment-based and community-lead Beaver Management Groups, in order to share knowledge, strategies and learning as we welcome beavers back to the wild. While we don't want to single them out as special and requiring extensive management or control, we do need to recognize they will have impacts and therefore need the systems in place to respond.

The social dimension

It has never been more important to recognize that nature's restoration relies on people and our interaction with the environment. The social dimension to beaver restoration is massive. A big part of what we do is outreach, communications and education on beaver coexistence and community-led conservation. We want people to believe in better, to strive for a vision of landscapes come alive and to feel integral to that vision. We have lost the memory of large herbivores in our landscape and beavers offer an opportunity to re-engage an audience beyond conservationists in nature's overall health and care.

Beavers also invite the conversation on land use, access, the state of our rivers and that the water cycle is everyone's business. More people need to know what happens in and around rivers. It should matter to them. Communities are often the last line of defence against damaging actions and we have found whole catchment beaver restoration can draw people together around a desire to rebuild their local ecosystems. with beavers.

The Beaver Code

As with all wildlife watching, beavers must be treated with respect and care. Beaver Trust has produced a Beaver Code, available online, offering basic guidance on how to look for and observe beavers in the wild. We should

- Be quiet – contribute to the peace and quiet along our rivers

- Know the signs – tell-tale clues as to beaver whereabouts

- Bring binoculars – especially in summer through lush vegetation they can be helpful

- Follow the path – straying can lead to the damage of potential refuge & feeding habitat

- Set a good example – we're all educating each other when it comes to observing wildlife sensibly

The Future of Conservation

We need young and old to become active conservationists, believing in a better future for our landscapes, to think big and have hope for nature's recovery. Beavers can help with this vision, but it is vital we all work together and give nature space to thrive. After all, we are nature and cannot sit back and watch its demise unscathed.

Eva Bishop, Communications Director.

www.beavertrust.org

Myths and Legends

While there are plenty of myths and legends about these unusual animals, they have also been responsible for seeding a considerable mystery. Erwin H. Barbour was the first palaeontologist to write about what were known as Devil's Corkscrews. Of these structures, some over 2 metres deep, that were found in the ground of Nebraska he said "Their forms are magnificent; their symmetry perfect; their organisation beyond my comprehension."

They appear in sandstone dating back to the Miocene, over 20 million years ago. Theories considered included that they were giant freshwater sponges, or the remains of root systems of plants. Careful examination of these amazing objects revealed that there were actually casts created from burrows

A. Daemonelix or "Devils corkscrews" in the Daemonelix beds near Harrison, Sioux county, Nebraska. Photograph by Barbour.

of rodents – an early beaver, busily engineering yet more amazing features, using its teeth to excavate rather than to fell.

As Rachel Poliquin points out, in her fascinating monograph on beaver iconography, where and when 'beaver' is mentioned will generate very different responses. The beaver has meant very different things to different people over the ages and around the world. It is easy to see why – a creature that defies the 'normal' order of things. Birds inhabit the air, fish the water and animals the land. Here is something

that is not a fish, yet lives in water. The extraordinary tail generates its own tall tales. It is related to the fishy nature of the animal, perhaps, and this is what was suggested by the eighteenth-century naturalist Comte de Buffon. Erroneously believing beavers ate fish it was argued that this had resulted in the animal becoming part fish.

This belief did grant a certain advantage to the strict adherents of religion, who were able to persuade themselves that on days of fasting, during which meat could not be eaten, the beaver was exempted due to its fishy nature. Beaver and chips on Friday, then. Interestingly a similar contorted logic was used by the Catholic missionaries to South

America when they came across the capybara.

It is not just for food that the beaver was of interest to humanity. The beaver has long been held to be the source of quite wonderful medicine.

Castoreum, the secretions of the beaver's scent organs, has been held as a powerful medicine since ancient times. The waxy exudate collects in 'castor sacs' and is used by both sexes for scent. Though for thousands of years it was 'known' that this valuable musk was to be found in a beaver's testicles.

So prevalent is the false story, that it pervaded a myth that was understood to be a truth since at least the sixth century BC when Aesop wrote: "It is said that when the beaver is being chased by dogs and realises that he cannot outrun them,

he bites off his testicles, since he knows that this is what he is hunted for. I suppose there is some kind of superhuman understanding that prompts the beaver to act in this way, for as soon as the hunter lays his hands on that magical medicine, he abandons the chase and calls off his dogs."

As Poliquin points out, it is deeply ironic that, 2000 years after this, rather than the beaver sacrificing his essence to save his skin, that very musk was being used as a lure to trap beavers for their skin.

This story then proved to be a very important component in the measure of the quality of the beaver's character. Animals were believed to have a god-given nature that we could devise – some animals crafty, some wise, some industrious. Well for the beaver their nature was considered a virtue.

Why was the castoreum so sought after? As a curative, it was blessed with many imagined properties. The reality is that castoreum can, indeed, contain therapeutic ingredients. Gnawing on willow will cause salicylic acid to be found there, and this is essentially aspirin. However, the amount to be squeezed from a beaver would not really touch a headache. Additionally, if Scots pine has been worked on there is a chance that phenol will be found, a chemical with some anaesthetic properties. Catechol, hydroquinone and benzoic acid have also been discovered in castoreum. But the quantities are small.

The Romans believed that burning castoreum would create fumes that

faciunt nequa tela obuium animal incimac.
Conflictis fortuito si quido pugnantur non
mediocrem hūt curam sauciorum. Nam fes
sos uulneratosep in medium receptant.

Est animal quod dr castor mansuetum
nimis. cuius testiculi medicine sunt ap
tissimi. de quo dicit phisiologus. quia cum
uenatorem se insequentem cognouerit: mor
su testiculos sibi abscidit. & in faciem uena

could cause an abortion. The range of cures castoreum could offer was considerable, including dealing with headaches, cramps, hysteria, nervousness and impotence. It is still available to buy on eBay from Siberia – though there is a disclaimer as to any possible curative qualities.

It is not just medicinal uses for which the beaver had to sacrifice its castoreum – the substance has also long been used in perfumes, and in food as a flavouring. There has to be a question as to how it was discovered that by squeezing the anal area of an animal, generating a substance with a bitter and rank odour, that this exudate when mixed with alcohol morphs into a something akin to vanilla.

The vanilla essence was not lost on food producers wanting to find a way to avoid the expensive natural vanilla pods – so castoreum became a component of sweet foods. This has rather diminished in scale, the process of anaesthetising and then 'milking' a beaver making it an extravagant source of flavour. It is still a permitted additive to foods, though the vast majority of all vanilla flavouring is now from the chemical vanillin – originally synthesised from a number of plants, including pine bark and clove oil. In the 1970s there was a further step away from the vanilla plant (and the beaver) when it was found how to synthesis the chemical via petrochemicals.

While many people looked on the beaver as a resource to be consumed, even in the height of the hunting era there were some who considered that they were worth more alive than dead. It is easy to patronise the Aboriginal Nations of North America with unconsidered assumptions about their desire to work with nature. In fact many, especially from the wet north east of the country were actively engaged in the beaver trade with the Europeans.

In the Great Plains, however, attitudes were different. As Rachel Poliquin writes, "...as fur traders made their way westward into the prairies they reported that the indigenous people, traditionally nomadic bison hunters, refused to kill beavers."

Why was this source of income ignored? This is where there is a fascinating collision between the practical and the sacred. Yes, plenty of anthropologists have talked of the sacred nature of the relationship, and it goes deep. Several tribes

from the Blackfoot Nations have a foundation myth of a world made by a giant beaver. Poliquin writes that, "Other groups claimed descent from beavers, and the Beaver Bundle was at the centre of the Blackfoot's most sacred ceremonies. Various legends surround the Beaver Bundle's spiritual origins, but most tell of a wandering or forsaken man or woman who is taken in by a beaver. The beaver eventually sends the wanderer back to his or her people with a precious gift: a bundle of objects with healing properties and powerful prayers, dances and songs to defend against death and disease."

It is possible this spiritual connection has very secular roots. A limiting feature to life on the prairies is water. Beavers store water in the ponds behind their dams; and in addition they also collect potential

BEAVER

An Alphabet of typical Specimens with 26 Illustrations, together with Notes and a terminal Essay on the manners and customs of Beavering Men

A magnificent Specimen of the Bald-King Beaver in full winter coat.

1/-

JOHN KETTELWELL

building materials and firewood. All of which can help in the survival of people. Therefore, while there was plenty of food available in the form of bison, the beavers were safe as their crucial role in human survival ensured their elevation to a sacred species. Unfortunately for the beaver the European hunters felt no such qualms.

Even the saving of Saint Felix of Burgundy from death by drowning failed to get them extra protection – not even a patron saint! The folk tale goes, related by Derek Gow, that Felix's ship was wrecked in a storm on the River Babingley in Norfolk in 615 AD. A colony of beavers rescued him from drowning and in gratitude the chief beaver was consecrated as a bishop. While the village is long gone, there is still a signpost recording the event, with a beaver

Village sign in Babingley. Phot by Uksignpix.

in bishop's regalia blessing another. In the early twentieth century, there was a dramatic addition to meanings of the word 'beaver' when it became popularised as a vulgar term for a woman's pubic hair. The origin of this transformation requires a little explanation. It emerged from a popular game called Beaver. The Associated Press, on October 5th, 1922, carried the following story.

"Lord and Lady Mountbatten – she is one of England's prettiest and richest women and he is King George's cousin – decided today they would go to the world's series [baseball] game and compare it with London's new outdoor sport – "beaver."

"Beaver" said Lord Mountbatten, "is a street game anyone can play. You walk along with a friend. If you spot a chap with a beard you call out 'Beaver'. That counts 15 points. If it is a white beard, this is 'polar beaver' and counts 30. You score as in tennis. The winners makes the loser buy the drinks. And it is driving beards right out of London."

Beards were clearly of note and earlier in the year the Columbia Evening Missourian wrote that, "The Hirsute Half-hundred, those whiskered gentry who astonished London a few weeks ago with their slogan, "A beard on the chin keeps the shaving money in," have now been eclipsed by the Cambridge University student society, which has sworn to wear beards forevermore and are known as the Beavers. One Beaver, who boasted a twelve-inch beard, had it pulled off in one of these rags to the disgust of his fellow Beavers, who found it was a spoof beard."

Nice Beaver!

Earlier still, in 1906, a book called *The Shaver's Calendar* stated that, "Everybody who knew anything at all about beards knows that a bearded man is technically a "beaver," while a beard is, to the expert, a "beaverage.""

The game of Beaver lead to the first ever recorded use of the slang term for pubic hair, in a limerick published in 1927.

There was a young lady name Eva
Who went to a ball as Godiva
But a change in the lights,
Showed a tear in her tights,
And a low fellow present yelled
"Beaver"

Which in turn generated one of the funniest moments in movie-making history in the 1988 film *Naked Gun*, when the actor Leslie Nielsen looked up at Priscilla Presley on the ladder in the attic and commented 'nice beaver' – just as she passes him a taxidermy specimen.

Wisdom & Creativity by P. Poitras-Jarrett.

Art, Literature and Advertising

It is perhaps fortunate that Robert Burns was unaware of the way in which the name for this animal might become (ab)used when he worked on this air – 'Cock up your Beaver'. His song is a rousing call to arms, about getting a feather (from a cock) to put in your (beaver) hat.

When first my brave Johnie lad came to this town,
He had a blue bonnet that wanted the crown,
But now he has gotten a hat and a feather –
Hey, brave Johnie lad, cock up your beaver!
Cock up your beaver, and cock it fu' sprush!
We'll over the border and gie them a brush:
There's somebody there we'll teach better behavior –
Hey, brave Johnie lad, cock up your beaver!

On safer ground, it is thanks in large part to CS Lewis and his *Chronicles of Narnia* that the beaver is 'known' as a piscivore; but as has been made clear, they are actually herbivorous and will not eat fish. In fact their very presence helps increase and maintain fish populations, so anglers have nothing to fear. Their role in the story is very much based on the perception of the wild animal, apart from their diet, of course. They are considered to be very upright and virtuous citizens.

For obvious reasons the beaver is not a regular in stories from Britain, its demise predating the flurry of animal-based children's stories in the twentieth century. Although perhaps there may yet be a resurgence, most stories to date have come from across the Atlantic.

87 Beavers Lost by Sarah Battensby.

Untitled, part of *87Beavers: In memoriam* by Fausteja Eglynaite.

The industriousness of Paddy the Beaver, from the 1917 book by Thornton W. Burgess, is clear to see from the opening lines:

"Work, work all the night
While the stars are shining bright;
Work, work all the day;
I have got no time to play."

This little rhyme Paddy the Beaver made up as he toiled at building the dam which was to make the pond he so much desired deep in the Green Forest.

A great proponent of the beaver in the 1930s was Grey Owl and his book, *The Adventures of Sajo and her Beaver People*, became a best seller. Grey Owl was a fascinating character, he presented himself as a Native American and protector of the Canadian wilderness. He rescued and raised beaver kits – following

his career as a fur trapper being upended by the persuasion of his 'informal' wife, Anahareo. He argued passionately for the protection of the forests many decades before the popular rise of environmentalism. Yet he was born Archibald Stansfield Belaney, in Hastings, in 1888, managing to maintain his fiction until his death in 1938.

Less sophisticated, there are comic book outings for beavers – *Space Beaver* by Darick Robertson has rather subverted the usual image of the animal; no longer diligent and virtuous, 'Beave' as the character is mostly known is a party animal, turned vigilante.

The less said about *Zombeavers*, well, probably the better – this 2014 horror comedy film featured, as the title suggests, zombie beavers.

Unsurprisingly, beavers also make it into the world of computer games. The Animal Crossing games feature both Chip and Chip Junior (CJ) but the designers have fallen at the first hurdle of biological accuracy, as CJ is deeply embedded within the fishing industry! The singer Justin Bieber was not amused at the creation of the character Joustin Beaver in a game that ended up in court. At least Sharky the Beaver has remained out of the courts, but trapped within an Augmented Reality game from 2012.

The beaver makes an unexpected appearance in the coat of arms for the City of Oxford. The central shield of the image has the visual pun of an ox fording a river – all well and good, but this shield is supported by a black elephant and a green beaver (right). These beasts are thought to have become entangled in the Oxford story due to their association with two members of the court of Elizabeth I who spent a week, as part of her summer progress in 1566, visiting the University of Oxford and staying at Christchurch College.

Other ceremonial beavers include Benny, the somewhat menacing mascot for Oregon State University, and Amik, the mascot when the 1976 Summer Olympics were held in Montreal, Canada, – Amik is the Algonquin for beaver. The beaver was chosen after a competition and because the animal is associated not just with Canada but also with hard work. The National Parks service of Canada has also unsurprisingly, adopted the beaver as a logo.

FORTIS EST VERITAS

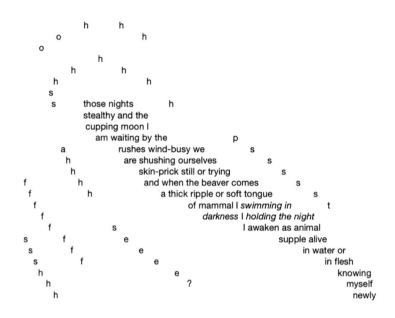

those nights
stealthy and the
cupping moon I
am waiting by the
rushes wind-busy we
are shushing ourselves
skin-prick still or trying
and when the beaver comes
a thick ripple or soft tongue
of mammal I *swimming in*
darkness I *holding the night*
I awaken as animal
supple alive
in water or
in flesh
knowing
myself
newly

Untitled poem, part of *87Beavers:*
In memoriam by Sophie Ramsay.

For many in the UK the closest they get to beavers at the moment is through the Scouting movement. The origin of the Beavers is actually from the Northern Ireland organisation that emerged in 1966 out of The Little Brothers. The Beavers were then picked up by the Scouts in Canada in 1974 and spread from there. Some countries embraced more common and local species, but the UK went with Beavers.

It would be lovely to think that this was a deeply prescient decision, a foreknowledge of the amazing things that are going to come with the return of this animal. There is so much to be gained from embracing the beaver as an ally in the building of a biodiverse land. If the UK is to meet its goals with regards to limiting the impacts of climate change, or increasing biodiversity and bioabundance, there is little to beat the beaver as the tool with which to achieve these results quickly and efficiently.

Beaver Museum, Brennilis, Brittany.

Castoro Cellars, California.

Beaver sculpture, over entrance to Centre Block of Canadian Parliament, Ottawa, Ontario, Canada, by D. Gordon E. Robertson.

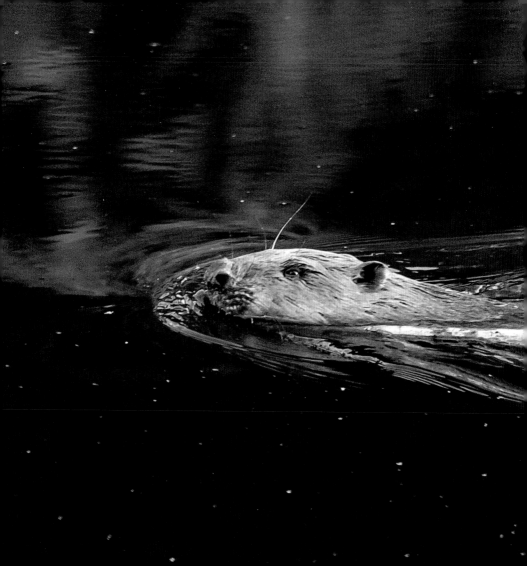

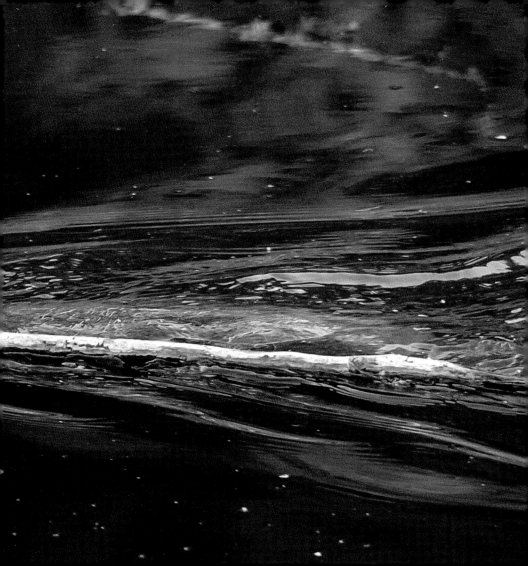

Photo credits and artworks

Front cover: Dod Morrison
Back cover left to right: Dod Morrison, Derek Gow , Colin Black, Elliot McCandless.

What is a beaver?

Pages 4, 20: Nick Upton
Page 7: Public domain
Pages 8, 10, 18, 21, 22: Dod Morrison
Page 9: Morgan Trimble / Alamy Stock Photo
Page 19: Minden Pictures / Alamy Stock Photo
Page 11: Colin Black
Page 13: Will Higgs: www.skullsite.co.uk
Pages 14, 16, 17, 24, 29: Elliot McCandless
Pages 15, 26-27, 28: Derek Gow
Pages 25: Hugh Warwick

Beaver Life

Pages 30, 32, 33, 38-39: Colin Black
Pages 34-35: Nick Upton
Pages 36: Dod Morrison
Pages 37: Derek Gow
Pages 40-41: Andy Coventry

Beaver Engineering

Pages 42, 44, 52-53, 54, 62-63, 64, 66 (bottom left): Elliot McCandless
Pages 45, 48, 56, 58-59, 66 (top photos and bottom right): Dod Morrison
Pages 46, 47, 50, 51, 57: Public domain
Pages 49, 61, 68: Derek Gow
Pages 55, 65: Nick Upton

People and Beavers

Pages 70, 73, 74, 76: Colin Black
Pages 75, 80: Dod Morrison
Pages 77, 83, 87: Derek Gow
Pages 78: Svetlana Savchenko
Pages 79: Olga Lozovskaya
Pages 84, 88: Public domain
Page 86: Pat Morris
Pages 89: Tameside Local Studies & Archives

Beaver Reintroductions

Pages 90, 93, 99, 102-103, 104, 107, 108, 110-111, 113, 115: Elliot McCandless
Pages 94-95: Andy Coventry
Page 96: Nick Upton
Page 100: Dod Morrison

Beaver Trust
Pages 116, 119, 125: Elliot McCandless
Pages 120-121, 126: Dod Morrison
Page 122: Hugh Warwick

Myths and Legends
Pages 130, 137: Bodleian Library
Page 132: Public domain
Page 133: Public domain
Page 134: Elliot McCandless
Page 135: Pat Morris
Page 140: Project Gutenberg
Page 141: Uksignpix
Pages 143: Hugh Warwick

Art, Literature and Advertising
Pages 144: P. Poitras-Jarrett
Pages 147: Sarah Battensby
Pages 148: Fausteja Eglynaite
Pages 151: Hugh Warwick
Pages 152: Sophie Ramsay
Pages 153: Derek Gow
Pages 154: Castoro Cellars
Pages 155: D. Gordon E. Robertson,
wikipedia, public domain
Pages 156-157: Dod Morrison
Pages 38–47: Dartmoo

Endpapers: linocut by Jane Russ

Every effort has been made to trace copyright holders of material and acknowledge permission for this publication. The publisher apologises for any errors or omissions to rights holders and would be grateful for notification of credits and corrections that should be included in future reprints or editions of this book.

Acknowledgements

My first encounter with beavers was thanks to Paul and Louise Ramsay at their amazing ecotourism venture on the Bamff estate. The work they have done in Perthshire is phenomenal and to visit is to be able to see the difference a few beavers can make to the land.

Derek Gow has also generously invited me into his corner of paradise at Rewilding Coombeshead in Devon. Enjoying a drink as the sun sets while watching beaver kits play is a true delight.

Eva Bishop is a remarkable dynamo at the heart of the Beaver Trust, she has been so generous with her time and support for this book.

Enormous thanks to the photographers, Nick Upton, Elliot McCandless, Colin Black, Pat Morris, Andy Coventry and Dod Morrison.

The artists from the 87Beavers: In Memoriam have been very generous in allowing me to use their images.

Svetlana Savchenko and Olga Lozovskaya helped provide images from the amazing archaeological work in Russia at short notice.

The Beaver Book
Published in Great Britain in 2021 by Graffeg Limited.

Written by Hugh Warwick copyright © 2021. Designed and produced by Graffeg Limited copyright © 2021.

Graffeg Limited, 24 Stradey Park Business Centre, Mwrwg Road, Llangennech, Llanelli, Carmarthenshire, SA14 8YP, Wales, UK. Tel: 01554 824000. www.graffeg.com.

Hugh Warwick is hereby identified as the author of this work in accordance with section 77 of the Copyrights, Designs and Patents Act 1988.

A CIP Catalogue record for this book is available from the British Library.

All rights reserved. No part of this publication may be reproduced, stored in a retrieval system or transmitted, in any form or by any means, electronic, mechanical, photocopying, recording or otherwise, without the prior permission of the publishers.

The publisher acknowledges the financial support of the Books Council of Wales. www.gwales.com.

ISBN 9781914079214

1 2 3 4 5 6 7 8 9

MIX
Paper from responsible sources
FSC® C014138

Books in the series

The Hare Book

The Fox Book

The Owl Book

The Red Squirrel Book

The Hedgehog Book

The Bee Book

The Robin Book

The Badger Book

The Puffin Book

The Native Pony Book

The Beaver Book

www.graffeg.com

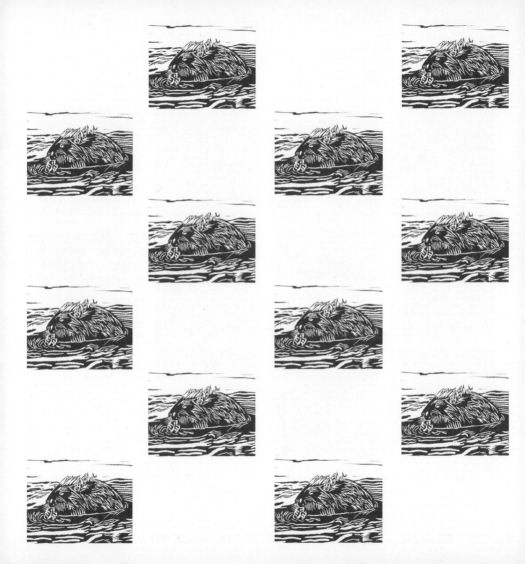